POP BUCHANAN

InvestAI: Inference Chips

How NVIDIA, Amazon, Tesla, and the AI Giants Are Racing to Control Hardware, Power, and Scale

First published by Invest AI 2026

Disclaimer

This book is provided for educational, informational, and general interest purposes only. Nothing in this book should be construed as financial, investment, legal, or tax advice, nor as a recommendation to buy, sell, or hold any security, asset, or investment strategy. InvestAI, Invest AI, and Pop Buchanan are not registered investment advisors, brokers, or fiduciaries. All ideas, frameworks, and discussions presented here are intended to explore future technology, infrastructure trends, and long-range economic possibilities in an analytical and conceptual manner. Readers are strongly encouraged to conduct their own research and consult with qualified financial professionals, including licensed fiduciaries, before making any investment decisions. Investing involves risk, including the possible loss of capital. InvestAI exists to help readers think more clearly about emerging technology, infrastructure, and long-term systems shaping the future, not to provide personalized financial guidance. Use this book as a lens for understanding, not as a substitute for professional advice.

First edition

This book was professionally typeset on Reedsy.
Find out more at reedsy.com

Contents

Preface iv
Introduction 1
1 What Inference Chips Are and Why They Matter 5
2 The Intelligence Illusion 10
3 Why Inference, Not Models, Decides Winners 14
4 Energy Is the First AI Constraint 17
5 Vertical Integration as Competitive Law 20
6 The Inference Infrastructure Stack 24
7 A Live Case Study in Vertical AI 27
8 What Can Break This Thesis 30
9 Mapping Investment Exposure by Layer 33
10 The AI Landscape in 2036 36
11 How Investors Read the Inference Era 39
12 Technologies That Shape the Road to 2036 42
13 The Invest AI Budget Stack: How Energy, Heat, Permission,... 45
14 Appendix: The Invest AI Inference Infrastructure Question... 49
15 Conclusion 73

Preface

For most of modern history, power came from what you could extract.

Oil. Coal. Steel. Land.

Later, power came from what you could connect.

Networks. Software. Platforms. Attention.

Artificial intelligence looks, at first, like the next chapter in that same story. Smarter systems. Better algorithms. Faster progress. Louder announcements.

But something different is happening underneath the noise.

The companies shaping the future of AI are no longer competing primarily on intelligence. They are competing on whether intelligence can be run everywhere, all the time, without collapsing under its own weight.

This race is already underway.

NVIDIA does not sell intelligence. It sells the silicon that makes intelligence possible at scale. Every breakthrough model still has to run somewhere, and most of them run on NVIDIA hardware. That quiet dependency is not an accident. It is the foundation of an empire built on inference.

Amazon does not need to win the AI branding war. It needs AI to run cheaply, reliably, and nonstop inside its cloud, its logistics network, its warehouses, and its retail systems. Custom chips, energy efficiency, and control over deployment matter more to Amazon than who has the flashiest model.

Tesla does not treat AI as software. It treats it as a physical system that must operate inside vehicles, robots, factories, and energy products. Decisions cannot wait for distant servers. Intelligence has to live at the edge, embedded in hardware, constrained by heat, power, and safety.

Google and Microsoft are building their own silicon not because they love hardware, but because renting intelligence forever is a losing proposition. Whoever controls inference controls margins, reliability, and long-term leverage.

Even space has entered the equation.

SpaceX has shown that deployment is not just about servers and data centers. Launch, orbit, and global coverage collapse distance. Satellites are not just communication tools. They are moving compute surfaces. Intelligence does not have to stay on the ground.

None of these companies are following the same playbook. But they are converging on the same truth.

Artificial intelligence is not free to scale.

Every intelligent action costs energy.

Every intelligent system produces heat.

Every intelligent decision must happen fast enough to matter.

Every intelligent machine must exist somewhere in the physical world.

As AI spreads into cars, robots, factories, cities, satellites, and infrastructure, these constraints stop being technical details and start becoming governing forces.

This is where the future gets decided.

Not by who has the smartest demo.

Not by who announces the next model first. But by who can power intelligence at scale, cool it, deploy it, and keep it running when demand never shuts off.

This book is written for investors who sense that something fundamental has shifted but have not yet been given a clear map.

It is not a traditional Invest AI investing book. It does not offer stock tips or short-term trades. It does not try to predict quarterly earnings or hype the next announcement. It is part investment analysis, part systems thinking, and part future-forward landscape.

The goal is orientation.

To understand why inference chips sit at the center of the AI economy.

To see why energy, hardware, and deployment quietly govern intelligence.

To recognize why the companies racing ahead all start to look structurally similar, even when their businesses appear unrelated.

To think in decades instead of headlines.

Whether intelligence runs in data centers, vehicles, underground facilities, orbiting satellites, or places not yet imagined is less important than this single question.

Who can afford to run it everywhere.

The chapters that follow strip away hype and personalities. They focus on the machinery beneath the narrative. They explain why the AI era is not won by intelligence alone, but by the infrastructure that allows intelligence to exist in the real world.

The race is already happening.

This book explains what it is really about.

Introduction

When people talk about artificial intelligence, they usually talk about models. They talk about how smart a system is, how it was trained, and what it can do. From an investment standpoint, that is not where the real leverage is.

The real leverage is in the chips.

Artificial intelligence only works when it runs. Every answer, every image, every recommendation, and every decision an AI system makes must be executed on hardware. That execution is called inference, and the hardware that performs it is called an inference chip.

Inference is not learning. Inference is using what has already been learned.

Every time you type into ChatGPT and receive a response, an inference chip is doing the work. The model was trained earlier, somewhere else, often long before you asked your question. In that moment, the system is simply running the model fast enough to respond to you. That run consumes electricity. It produces heat. It happens on silicon.

That silicon is the product.

An inference chip is a processor designed to run trained AI models efficiently, repeatedly, and with minimal delay. It is built for speed, reliability, and scale. Training chips teach models. Inference chips keep models alive in the real world.

Inference chips sit everywhere intelligence touches daily life.

They power chat systems and search engines in data centers.

They sit inside vehicles that must make driving decisions every second.

They run robots in factories and warehouses.

They operate cameras, sensors, phones, satellites, and energy systems.

Inference chips are always on. That is what makes them different.

Training happens occasionally. Inference happens constantly. Because inference never stops, the cost of running it becomes the real business problem. As AI spreads, inference demand explodes. More users. More machines. More decisions per second.

This is why inference chips become infrastructure.

From an investment perspective, this is the pivot point. The question is no longer who has the smartest model. The question is who controls the hardware that runs intelligence everywhere, cheaply and reliably, for years at a time.

Today, one company dominates inference chips at scale. That dominance matters because whoever controls inference chips controls the cost of AI.

But this will not remain static.

As inference demand grows, companies seek independence. Some build competing hardware to lower costs. Others design custom chips to run AI internally. Vehicles and robots require inference locally, without waiting on distant data centers. Custom chips make that possible.

The pattern is consistent. The companies that expect to run AI nonstop are moving toward owning inference chips instead of renting them.

This is where inference chips connect directly to infrastructure.

Inference chips do not exist in isolation. They require electricity, cooling, manufacturing capacity, supply chains, and physical deployment. They must be produced in large volumes. They must survive heat. They must operate within power limits. They must be placed close to where decisions happen.

That is why scaling inference chips becomes difficult.

As inference demand grows, constraints pile up. Power grids strain. Data centers overheat. Manufacturing timelines stretch. Supply chains tighten. What began as a software challenge becomes an industrial one.

This is where the next decade will be decided.

The company or ecosystem that can design inference chips, manufacture them at scale, power them cheaply, cool them efficiently, and deploy them everywhere gains a compounding advantage. Their AI runs cheaper. Their margins improve. Their competitors hit limits sooner.

By 2036, artificial intelligence will not be limited by how smart models are. It will be limited by how many inference chips can be powered, cooled, and deployed in the real world.

That is why inference chips are the backbone of AI infrastructure.

Understanding inference chips is the single most important step in understanding the AI investment landscape. Everything else in this book builds on that foundation.

The next chapter explains why inference chips turn energy into the central constraint and why power, not intelligence, becomes the true governor of AI at scale.

1

What Inference Chips Are and Why They Matter

Inference Chips: How AI Actually Runs

When people talk about artificial intelligence, they usually talk about models. They talk about how smart a system is, how it was trained, and what it can do. From an investment standpoint, that is not where the real leverage is.

The real leverage is in the chips.

Artificial intelligence only works when it runs. Every answer, every image, every recommendation, and every decision an AI system makes must be executed on hardware. That execution is called inference, and the hardware that performs it is called an inference chip.

Inference is not learning. Inference is using what has already been learned.

Every time you type into ChatGPT and receive a response, an inference chip is doing the work. The model was trained earlier, somewhere else, often long before you asked your question. In that moment, the system is simply running the model fast enough to respond to you. That run consumes electricity. It produces heat. It happens on silicon.

That silicon is the product.

An inference chip is a processor designed to run trained AI models efficiently, repeatedly, and with minimal delay. It is built for speed, reliability, and scale. Training chips teach models. Inference chips keep models alive in the real world.

Inference chips sit everywhere intelligence touches daily life.

They power chat systems and search engines in data centers.

They sit inside vehicles that must make driving decisions every second.

They run robots in factories and warehouses.

They operate cameras, sensors, phones, satellites, and energy systems.

Inference chips are always on. That is what makes them different.

Training happens occasionally. Inference happens constantly. Because inference never stops, the cost of running it becomes the real business problem. As AI spreads, inference demand explodes. More users. More machines. More decisions per second.

This is why inference chips become infrastructure.

From an investment perspective, this is the pivot point. The question is no longer who has the smartest model. The question is who controls the hardware that runs intelligence everywhere, cheaply and reliably, for years at a time.

Today, one company dominates inference chips at scale. That dominance matters because whoever controls inference chips controls the cost of AI.

But this will not remain static.

As inference demand grows, companies seek independence. Some build competing hardware to lower costs. Others design custom chips to run AI internally. Vehicles and robots require inference locally, without waiting on distant data centers. Custom chips make that possible.

The pattern is consistent. The companies that expect to run AI nonstop are moving toward owning inference chips instead of renting them.

This is where inference chips connect directly to infrastructure.

Inference chips do not exist in isolation. They require electricity, cooling, manufacturing capacity, supply chains, and physical deployment. They must be produced in large volumes. They must survive heat. They must operate within power limits. They must be placed close to where decisions happen.

That is why scaling inference chips becomes difficult.

As inference demand grows, constraints pile up. Power grids strain. Data centers overheat. Manufacturing timelines stretch. Supply chains tighten. What began as a software challenge becomes an industrial one.

This is where the next decade will be decided.

The company or ecosystem that can design inference chips, manufacture them at scale, power them cheaply, cool them efficiently, and deploy them everywhere gains a compounding advantage. Their AI runs cheaper. Their margins improve. Their competitors hit limits sooner.

By 2036, artificial intelligence will not be limited by how smart models are. It will be limited by how many inference chips can be powered, cooled, and deployed in the real world.

That is why inference chips are the backbone of AI infrastructure.

Understanding inference chips is the single most important step in understanding the AI investment landscape. Everything else in this book builds on that foundation.

The next chapter explains why inference chips turn energy into the central constraint and why power, not intelligence, becomes the true governor of AI at scale.

2

The Intelligence Illusion

The Intelligence Illusion

Most people think the AI race is about who has the smartest system. That idea feels right because it is easy to see. New models launch, scores go up, and demos look impressive. Headlines compare one system to another and declare a winner. For a short time, those differences matter.

Then they fade.

This has happened before in every major technology shift. Early leaders look unbeatable. Others catch up. Methods spread. Tools improve. What once felt rare becomes common. Intelligence follows the same path.

AI models are improving fast, but they are also moving closer together. Open systems learn from public research. Techniques spread across teams. Talent changes jobs. What one group figures out, others soon repeat. Over time, intelligence becomes cheaper and easier to access.

That does not mean intelligence stops mattering. It means it stops being scarce.

Scarcity is what decides winners.

In the early days of AI, intelligence looked like the main limit. Training large models was expensive and slow. Only a few groups could do it. That phase is ending. Training still costs money, but it happens in bursts. A model is trained, released, and later improved again. Training is episodic.

Real-world AI does not work that way. Real-world AI runs all the time.

Every time an AI answers a question, guides a robot, helps a car turn, or sorts a package, it is running inference. Inference is the act of using intelligence, not creating it. Inference is constant. It does not turn off.

This is where the illusion breaks.

If intelligence were the true limit, the race would be about who trains the biggest model. But once many systems become good enough, the problem changes. The real question becomes who can run intelligence everywhere, all the time, at the lowest cost.

That question has little to do with how smart a model is.

Inference needs electricity. It needs chips. It needs cooling.

It needs networks. It needs to live close to the real world so decisions happen fast. These needs do not shrink as models improve. They grow.

As intelligence becomes cheaper, inference becomes more expensive.

This is the part most analysis misses. Better models do not reduce the need for infrastructure. They increase it. When AI becomes useful, demand explodes. When demand explodes, limits appear in power grids, factories, supply chains, and physical deployment.

This is why intelligence alone cannot decide the AI race.

When models converge, advantage moves elsewhere. It moves to systems that can deliver intelligence at scale. It moves to those who own the physical layers that make AI usable in the real world.

Software still matters, but software without infrastructure hits a wall.

The old story said the smartest system would win. The emerging reality says the most deployable system wins. The cheapest inference wins. The system closest to reality wins.

Once this is clear, many things start to make sense. Energy becomes central again. Hardware matters again. Manufacturing matters again. Distribution matters again.

Intelligence is becoming abundant. The ability to use it is not.

That is the illusion this book breaks.

The next chapter explains why inference replaces intelligence as the real bottleneck and why control of inference becomes the deciding factor in the AI era.

3

Why Inference, Not Models, Decides Winners

Once intelligence stops being scarce, something else takes its place. That thing is inference.

Inference is what happens after a model is built. It is the moment intelligence is used in the real world. Every answer, every movement, every decision an AI system makes is inference. It is not a one-time event. It is constant.

This difference matters.

Training a model happens in stages. A system is trained, tested, released, and later updated. Training is expensive, but it is occasional. Inference never stops. If an AI system is useful, it must run all day, every day, across many places at once.

Because inference never stops, it consumes resources nonstop.

It uses electricity every second. It uses hardware that must stay cool and reliable. It depends on networks that move data quickly. It needs to be close to where decisions happen so it does not lag behind reality. These needs turn inference into a physical problem, not just a software one.

This is why inference becomes the bottleneck.

As models improve, more people want to use them. As more people use them, inference demand grows. As inference demand grows, costs rise. Power bills increase. Hardware wears out. Data centers strain. Networks slow down. The system hits limits that better software alone cannot fix.

Inference cost becomes the real margin.

Two companies can use similar models and get very different results. The difference is not intelligence. It is how cheaply and widely they can run that intelligence. One company rents compute at high prices. Another owns its hardware, energy, and deployment. Over time, that gap compounds.

Inference also has to live close to the world.

A robot cannot wait seconds for a response. A vehicle cannot pause while data travels far away. A factory cannot stop because a cloud server is busy. Inference that lives too far from the action fails. This pushes intelligence outward, toward the edge, where people, machines, and environments exist.

Edge inference changes everything.

Instead of one central brain, intelligence spreads across devices, machines, vehicles, and networks. Each location needs its own compute, power, and connectivity. The system becomes larger, heavier, and more physical.

This is why inference favors infrastructure owners.

Owning inference means owning the conditions that make AI usable. It means controlling power, chips, placement, and scale. These are not abstract advantages. They are built over years. They require factories, logistics, and capital.

Models can be copied. Infrastructure cannot be copied quickly.

As inference becomes the center of value, the AI race stops looking like a software contest. It starts looking like an infrastructure buildout. The winners are not the ones with the smartest ideas. They are the ones who can deliver intelligence everywhere at the lowest cost.

This shift explains why energy, hardware, and deployment move to the center of the story. It explains why AI companies begin to look like industrial companies. It explains why vertical integration returns as a competitive advantage.

Inference is where intelligence meets reality. Reality has limits.

Whoever controls inference controls how far AI can go.

4

Energy Is the First AI Constraint

Every AI system runs on energy. Without power, intelligence does nothing.

This sounds obvious, but it is often ignored. Most AI discussion stays in the world of software, where limits feel abstract. Energy is not abstract. It is physical. It must be generated, stored, moved, and paid for.

Inference makes this clear.

Because inference runs all the time, it draws power all the time. Every answer costs electricity. Every movement costs electricity. As AI spreads into vehicles, robots, factories, and networks, energy demand grows nonstop.

This turns energy into the first real constraint.

Power grids were not built for always-on intelligence. They were built for homes, offices, and predictable industry. AI changes that pattern. It creates constant, heavy load in places that were not designed for it. Data centers already push local grids to their limits. Edge devices multiply the problem across entire regions.

When energy becomes scarce or unstable, AI slows down.

No amount of software can fix a power shortage. No algorithm can run without electricity. If energy is expensive, inference becomes expensive. If energy is unreliable, AI becomes unreliable.

This is why energy cost shapes AI margins.

Two systems can run the same intelligence and get very different outcomes. One pays high prices for power and struggles with outages. The other controls its energy supply and storage. Over time, the second system wins, even if its software is no better.

Energy storage matters as much as energy generation.

AI does not only need power. It needs stable power. Storage smooths spikes, protects uptime, and lowers costs. Without storage, systems break under demand. With storage, systems scale.

This turns energy into strategy.

As AI demand grows, energy stops being a background utility and becomes a competitive weapon. Systems that control power, storage, and delivery gain an advantage that software alone cannot match.

This is also why AI pushes toward new locations.

Some regions cannot support more load. Others can. AI follows cheap, stable energy. Over time, intelligence clusters around power, not talent.

Energy does not care about hype or timelines. It moves slowly. It takes years to build capacity. Once built, it shapes everything on top of it.

This is why energy comes before intelligence.

Until power is solved, AI cannot scale freely. Every model, every inference system, every deployment runs into the same wall. Energy is the wall.

The next chapter explains why vertical integration becomes the way around that wall and why owning the stack matters more than renting it.

5

Vertical Integration as Competitive Law

When systems become complex, coordination matters more than optimization.

AI has reached that stage.

Running intelligence at scale is no longer a single problem. It is many problems stacked on top of each other. Power must be available. Hardware must exist. Manufacturing must keep pace. Deployment must be reliable. Data must flow back into the system. When these layers are owned by different parties, friction appears everywhere.

That friction costs time, money, and control.

Vertical integration is the response to that friction. It is not a philosophy. It is a survival strategy.

In a fragmented system, each layer answers to a different

incentive. Energy providers optimize for the grid. Hardware vendors optimize for sales cycles. Cloud platforms optimize for utilization. Software teams optimize for features. None of them optimize for the whole.

As AI demand grows, the gaps between these layers widen.

Latency increases because systems are too far apart. Costs rise because every layer takes a margin. Reliability suffers because responsibility is split. When something breaks, no one owns the full failure.

Vertical integration reduces those gaps.

When one system controls energy, hardware, deployment, and software together, decisions improve. Tradeoffs become internal. Costs drop because margins collapse inward. Latency shrinks because systems are designed to work together, not patched together.

This is not new. It has happened before in other industries.

When electricity spread, companies that controlled generation and distribution dominated. When computing scaled, companies that controlled chips and systems gained leverage. AI follows the same pattern because it depends on physical reality.

Coordination beats specialization when the system runs nonstop.

AI inference cannot pause while contracts renegotiate. It cannot wait for vendors to align incentives. It cannot afford downtime caused by misaligned layers. The system either works as one or it fails in pieces.

Ownership beats access.

Renting infrastructure works when demand is low and flexible. It breaks when demand is constant and critical. As inference becomes essential, reliance on external layers becomes a risk. Control replaces convenience.

This is why AI companies begin to look less like software startups and more like industrial platforms. They invest in power. They build hardware. They control deployment. They collapse distance between decision and action.

Vertical integration does not guarantee success. It increases responsibility and capital needs. But in a world where inference never stops, fragmentation becomes more dangerous than scale.

This is not about building everything in-house for its own sake. It is about reducing the number of handoffs between intelligence and reality.

As AI moves deeper into the physical world, the systems that survive are the ones that can act as a single organism. They sense, decide, and act without negotiating with themselves.

Vertical integration becomes less of a choice and more of a competitive law.

The next chapter lays out the full inference infrastructure stack and shows how these layers fit together as a single system.

6

The Inference Infrastructure Stack

Once inference becomes the center of value, the system around it becomes clear. AI does not live in one place. It moves through layers. Each layer supports the one above it. If any layer breaks, the system weakens.

This is the inference infrastructure stack.

At the base of the stack is energy. Every AI action begins with power. Without steady electricity, nothing runs. Energy sets the ceiling for everything else. Cheap, stable power allows inference to expand. Expensive or unstable power forces limits.

Above energy sits compute silicon. These are the chips that turn power into decisions. They must be fast, efficient, and reliable. As inference grows, general-purpose hardware becomes too slow or too costly. Systems move toward specialized chips designed for constant use.

Manufacturing comes next. Chips, servers, batteries, robots, and devices must be built at scale. Design alone is not enough. If factories cannot produce fast enough, growth stalls. Manufacturing speed becomes a form of leverage.

Deployment follows manufacturing. Intelligence must be placed where it is needed. This includes data centers, edge devices, vehicles, robots, and satellites. Deployment decides latency. The closer inference is to the real world, the better it performs.

Distribution connects everything. Networks move data, updates, and coordination across the system. Distribution turns isolated intelligence into a shared capability. Without strong distribution, intelligence stays local and limited.

At the top of the stack is data feedback. Every action creates information. That information flows back into the system to improve performance, reduce errors, and refine decisions. Feedback closes the loop and allows the system to learn from reality, not just theory.

This stack works as a whole.

Energy without deployment does nothing. Hardware without manufacturing stays on paper. Deployment without distribution stays isolated. Data without feedback loses value. Each layer depends on the others.

This is why the stack favors integrated systems.

When one organization controls multiple layers, the system

becomes tighter. Costs fall because margins collapse inward. Performance improves because layers are designed together. Scaling becomes smoother because bottlenecks are visible early.

When layers are split across many owners, the stack weakens. Costs rise. Latency grows. Failures become harder to trace. Growth slows because no one controls the full path from power to action.

The inference infrastructure stack explains why AI is shifting away from pure software. It explains why physical assets return to the center of strategy. It explains why long-term advantage forms slowly, then compounds.

This stack is not tied to any single company. It is a structural model. Any system that wants to run intelligence everywhere must confront it.

Understanding this stack is the key to understanding the AI era. It shows where value is created, where it leaks, and where durable advantage forms.

The next chapter applies this stack to a real-world system in motion, not as a prediction, but as evidence of how the structure works when it is actively built.

7

A Live Case Study in Vertical AI

The inference stack is not theoretical. Pieces of it are already operating together in the real world.

One visible example comes from the group of companies often associated with Elon Musk. These companies matter here not because of a person, but because they show what happens when multiple layers of the inference stack are built at the same time.

SpaceX demonstrates what control over deployment looks like. Reusable rockets lower the cost of moving hardware into orbit and doing it often. Launch becomes routine instead of rare. When deployment costs fall, experimentation rises and scale follows.

Starlink shows how distribution becomes a computational surface. A satellite network is not just a way to move data. It places compute, routing, and decision-making closer to users, machines, and remote environments. This turns connectivity into part of the inference system.

Tesla illustrates edge inference at scale. Millions of vehicles run custom hardware that makes decisions in real time. Each vehicle acts as a mobile inference node. Power, compute, deployment, and data feedback operate together, not as separate services.

xAI represents model ownership and compute control. Training and inference are kept closer to the hardware and energy that support them. This reduces dependence on rented infrastructure and shortens the loop between development and deployment.

Energy storage and grid-scale batteries tie the system together. Stable power supports constant inference. Storage smooths demand and protects uptime. Without this layer, the rest of the system strains under load.

Taken together, these elements map cleanly onto the inference infrastructure stack. Energy supports compute. Compute feeds deployment. Deployment connects through distribution. Distribution generates data. Data improves performance. Each layer strengthens the others.

This is not a single merger and it does not need to be. Functional integration can exist through contracts, shared design goals, and aligned incentives. What matters is that the system behaves like one organism, even if it is made of separate parts.

This case study also shows the risks.

Building across many layers increases complexity. Capital

needs rise. Execution mistakes become costly. Regulation becomes unavoidable. If leadership changes or coordination fails, progress slows.

Yet even with those risks, the structure itself remains powerful. The advantage does not disappear if one company stumbles or leadership changes. The stack still favors whoever controls more layers more tightly than their competitors.

This is the lesson of the case study.

The value is not in any single product or announcement. It is in the direction of the build. The system moves toward lower inference cost, wider deployment, and tighter feedback. That direction creates compounding advantage over time.

The case study is evidence, not a promise. It shows how vertical AI looks when it is attempted in the real world. It also shows why the race shifts away from models and toward infrastructure.

The next chapter examines what could break this structure and where the thesis could fail.

8

What Can Break This Thesis

No framework is complete without its limits. If this thesis were guaranteed, it would already be priced in. The future never moves in straight lines, especially when technology, capital, and governments collide.

The first risk comes from regulation. When systems grow large enough to touch energy, communication, transportation, and defense, oversight follows. Governments may decide that too much control in one stack is unsafe. Rules can force separation, limit data sharing, or slow deployment. These actions do not destroy infrastructure advantage, but they can weaken coordination and stretch timelines.

Another risk comes from re-centralization. Large cloud platforms could push back. If centralized data centers become cheap enough, efficient enough, and well powered enough, they could reclaim inference from the edge. This would require major breakthroughs in energy pricing, cooling, and latency management. It is possible, but it demands changes across many physical systems at once.

A deeper risk comes from a true shift in computing itself. If a new form of computation drastically lowers energy use or hardware needs, the current stack could lose relevance. This would not happen overnight. Physical transitions take time. Factories, grids, and supply chains do not turn on a dime. Even so, a real breakthrough could reset the field.

Geopolitics adds another layer of uncertainty. Nations may fragment AI infrastructure along borders. Systems that work globally today could be forced to operate regionally tomorrow. This would not eliminate the thesis, but it would change its shape. Instead of one dominant stack, there could be several regional ones, each built around the same constraints.

There is also execution risk. Building across energy, hardware, manufacturing, and deployment is hard. Mistakes compound. Delays stack. Capital can be misallocated. Vertical integration increases responsibility. When something fails, there is no vendor to blame.

Finally, there is the risk of time itself. Infrastructure takes years to build. Markets can lose patience. Leadership can change. Priorities can shift. A strategy that is correct may still fail if it cannot survive long enough to matter.

These risks do not invalidate the thesis. They define its boundaries.

The core idea remains intact. Intelligence commoditizes.

Inference stays physical. Energy, hardware, and deployment shape outcomes. What changes is how fast the system moves and who is allowed to build it.

This chapter exists to keep the framework honest. It reminds us that advantage is not destiny. Structure matters, but so do politics, execution, and patience.

The next chapter moves from theory to application. It shows how this framework translates into real investment exposure, not as predictions, but as ways to think clearly about where value can compound and where it cannot.

9

Mapping Investment Exposure by Layer

Once the structure is clear, the question changes. The question is no longer who will win. The question becomes where value can compound even if the story changes.

This framework separates investment exposure by how close it sits to inference and how dependent it is on a single outcome. The closer an investment is to running inference in the real world, the higher the potential reward and the higher the risk. The farther it is, the steadier it becomes.

The first category is direct exposure. This includes companies that own and operate inference in live environments. These systems combine software, hardware, energy, and deployment. They run intelligence inside vehicles, robots, factories, networks, or large platforms. When they work, they scale fast and gain strong leverage. When they fail, losses can be sharp. These investments depend on execution, regulation, and capital discipline. They offer the most upside, but they demand the most conviction.

The second category is derivative exposure. These companies do not run inference themselves, but they enable it. They build the chips, batteries, automation systems, tools, and components that inference systems require. Their customers may change, but demand for their products grows as inference spreads. These businesses benefit from the overall direction of AI infrastructure without needing to pick a single winner. Their returns are usually steadier and less tied to headlines.

The third category is picks and shovels. These companies provide the basic materials and systems that make large-scale inference possible. Power equipment, cooling systems, grid components, industrial materials, logistics, and launch services fall into this group. They sit at the base of the stack. They rarely move fast, but they endure. Even if AI narratives shift, these systems remain necessary.

This layered view matters because it avoids false precision. Trying to predict the dominant AI company years in advance is risky. Understanding which layers must grow regardless of branding is more reliable.

As inference expands, all three layers benefit, but in different ways. Direct exposure captures speed and leverage. Derivative exposure captures scale and spread. Picks and shovels capture durability.

This is not about choosing one layer over another. It is about understanding what kind of risk is being taken and why. A balanced approach recognizes that infrastructure builds slowly, then compounds. It also recognizes that stories change faster than physical systems.

This framework allows investors to stay grounded. Instead of reacting to every new model or announcement, attention stays on power, deployment, and cost. These factors change slowly and reveal direction early.

Inference infrastructure is not a trade. It is a build cycle.

The final chapter looks ahead, not to make predictions, but to describe what this structure produces over time and how the AI landscape may look once inference becomes a permanent part of the world.

10

The AI Landscape in 2036

By 2036, the AI conversation will sound different. The excitement around new models will still exist, but it will no longer drive the center of the market. Intelligence will be assumed. Access will not.

AI will be everywhere, but it will not be evenly distributed. Some systems will run constantly, cheaply, and close to the real world. Others will exist mostly on paper, limited by cost, latency, or power. The gap between these two groups will define the era.

There will be fewer true AI winners.

As inference infrastructure becomes harder to build, only a small number of systems will control it at scale. These systems will look less like software companies and more like utilities. They will manage power, hardware, deployment, and networks as a single operation. Their advantage will not come from being smarter. It will come from being cheaper, closer, and more reliable.

Infrastructure moats will deepen.

Once energy, manufacturing, and deployment are in place, they are hard to replace. New competitors will face long timelines and high costs. Catching up will require years, not months. This will slow disruption and favor incumbents who built early.

AI will fragment by region.

Global systems will give way to regional ones. Energy policy, regulation, and national security will shape where inference can run. Some regions will build tightly integrated stacks. Others will rely on imports or rented capacity. The same framework will repeat in different forms around the world.

Inference will begin to feel like public infrastructure.

Just as electricity and the internet faded into the background, inference will become expected. People will not think about it directly. They will notice it only when it fails. Systems that provide steady, invisible intelligence will hold the most power.

The role of intelligence itself will shrink in the narrative.

Models will still improve, but they will no longer define leadership. The question will not be who is smartest, but who can deliver intelligence safely, cheaply, and everywhere it is needed. The story will move from invention to operation.

This does not mean innovation stops. It means innovation shifts.

The most important advances will happen in energy efficiency, hardware design, deployment methods, and system coordination. These advances will be quieter than model launches, but more important.

By 2036, the winners of the AI era will not look surprising in hindsight. They will be the ones who treated inference as a physical system early, invested in infrastructure patiently, and understood that intelligence without delivery is unfinished.

This book was written to make that outcome easier to see.

The AI era is not about thinking machines. It is about systems that can act in the real world, at scale, for a long time. Whoever controls that capability shapes what comes next.

11

How Investors Read the Inference Era

Investors often ask the wrong question first. They ask which company will win. That question feels practical, but it hides risk. Winning changes shape over time. Structures last longer than stories.

The inference era rewards investors who understand where value must live, not where attention happens to be.

The first shift investors must make is moving away from model comparison. Model quality changes fast. Public benchmarks move. Announcements pile up. None of this tells you who controls inference at scale. A system can be impressive and still uninvestable if it cannot deploy cheaply and reliably.

The second shift is understanding cost, not capability. Inference is not about how well a system performs once. It is about how much it costs to perform forever. Systems that depend on rented power, rented chips, and rented deployment inherit rising costs. Systems that control those layers compress cost over time.

Investors should look for ownership, not access.

Ownership shows up in boring places. Power contracts. Manufacturing timelines. Hardware design choices. Deployment density. These details matter more than product demos. They tell you whether inference costs will fall or rise.

Another mistake investors make is focusing only on speed. Fast growth without infrastructure breaks. Inference systems under strain reveal themselves through outages, rising expenses, and shrinking margins. Durable systems grow slower at first and then stabilize.

Inference also rewards patience.

Infrastructure compounds quietly. It does not reprice every quarter. Markets often underestimate it because the benefits are delayed. When the system finally clicks, it looks sudden, but it was built slowly.

The most useful investor question becomes simple. Does this system make inference cheaper over time or more expensive. Everything else follows.

This framework also helps investors avoid false confidence. No one needs to predict the dominant company. Instead, they can allocate across layers. Some exposure can sit close to inference. Some can sit behind it. Some can sit underneath it.

The goal is not certainty. The goal is resilience.

Inference infrastructure is not a trade. It is a cycle. Investors who understand that stop chasing headlines and start tracking physical reality.

That is how position is built in the inference era.

12

Technologies That Shape the Road to 2036

The path to 2036 will not be defined by a single breakthrough. It will be shaped by slow changes that stack on top of each other. These changes matter because they lower the cost of inference or expand where it can live.

One of the most important areas is energy efficiency. Every improvement in how much intelligence can be run per unit of power extends the system. Better cooling, better power conversion, and better storage quietly increase capacity without new generation.

Hardware specialization also continues. General chips give way to purpose-built ones. These chips are not smarter. They are cheaper to run and easier to deploy at scale. That shift favors systems that design for inference from the start.

Manufacturing automation plays a role as well. Faster factories reduce bottlenecks. More consistent output lowers risk.

Manufacturing speed becomes part of competitive advantage because it controls how fast inference capacity can grow.

Deployment methods evolve. Intelligence spreads into places it could not live before. Vehicles, machines, infrastructure, and remote environments become inference nodes. The closer intelligence gets to action, the more valuable it becomes.

Networks change alongside deployment. Distribution becomes denser and more resilient. Systems rely less on long-distance calls and more on local decision making. This lowers latency and reduces load on centralized systems.

Some technologies may amplify this trend further. New materials could improve energy storage. Better sensors could expand data feedback. Improved coordination systems could allow large fleets of machines to act together.

None of these changes break the thesis. They reinforce it.

They all push intelligence outward. They all increase demand for power, hardware, and deployment. They all reward systems that planned for physical scale early.

By 2036, the winning systems will not feel futuristic. They will feel obvious. They will look like infrastructure because they are infrastructure.

The mistake is thinking the future arrives through surprise. In reality, it arrives through accumulation.

The technologies that matter most are the ones that quietly make inference cheaper, closer, and more reliable. Everything else is decoration.

13

The Invest AI Budget Stack: How Energy, Heat, Permission, and Reality Decide the Future of AI

By 2036, artificial intelligence will not fail because it is not smart enough. It will fail because it breaks its own limits.

Every system that runs intelligence at scale lives inside budgets. These budgets are not financial. They are physical and social. When any one of them is exceeded, the system degrades, slows, or collapses.

This is the future frame that brings everything together.

The first budget is energy. Intelligence cannot exist without power. Every decision costs electricity. As inference spreads, energy demand becomes constant and heavy. Systems that cannot secure stable, cheap power hit a ceiling early.

The second budget is thermal. Every watt of power becomes

heat. Heat is not a side effect. It is the tax paid for intelligence. When heat builds faster than it can be managed, systems throttle, fail, or shut down. Cooling becomes as important as compute. Thermal stability becomes a form of uptime.

The third budget is regulatory. As AI controls more of the real world, permission matters. Systems must prove safety, reliability, and control. Intelligence that cannot be governed cannot be deployed at scale. The right to operate becomes as valuable as the ability to operate.

The fourth budget is reality. Intelligence that cannot verify the world drifts. Models hallucinate. Systems compound errors. Closed-loop feedback becomes essential. The system must sense, act, observe, and correct itself continuously.

These four budgets form a stack. Energy sits at the base. Thermal sits on top of energy. Regulation wraps the system. Reality closes the loop.

This is the Veste AI Budget Stack.

It explains why inference infrastructure matters. It explains why quantum computing matters without replacing classical systems. It explains why robotics, satellites, energy storage, and manufacturing converge. It explains why the future favors systems that feel boring, stable, and invisible.

This frame also reveals what most people miss.

Cooling is not just about removing heat. It is about preventing heat from forming in the wrong places at the wrong times. The future of thermal control is not bigger fans or colder liquids. It is prediction, scheduling, and behavior.

Heat is information.

A system that knows when heat will form can move workloads before failure. It can slow safely instead of crashing. It can trade speed for survival. This is thermal intelligence, not thermal brute force.

This is where the next layer of infrastructure is built. Not in the model. Not even in the chip alone. But in the control systems that manage energy and heat as first-class signals.

This book focused on inference because inference is where intelligence meets reality. The next book goes deeper into the budgets that decide whether inference survives.

Quantum computing fits into this future as an optimizer, not a replacement. It helps solve complex energy flows, routing problems, materials design, and system coordination. It accelerates the infrastructure. It does not run the world by itself.

The period from 2020 to 2036 is not about smarter machines. It is about building systems that can operate continuously without breaking their budgets.

That is the real future.

This chapter is not a conclusion. It is a handoff. It closes the inference framework and opens the next one. The Budget Stack is the lens through which the next phase of Invest AI will be built.

Inference makes intelligence useful. Budgets decide whether it lasts.

That is where the work continues.

14

Appendix: The Invest AI Inference Infrastructure Question Set: 40 Foundational Questions on Chips, Energy, Scale, and the AI Economy

By the time you reach this appendix, you have already moved past the surface conversation around artificial intelligence. You have seen how models converge, how inference chips turn energy into a governing constraint, how infrastructure compounds, and why control of hardware, power, and deployment ultimately decides scale. What remains is context.

This appendix exists to complete the picture.

Invest AI is written for readers who want more than headlines. Some arrive as investors. Others as operators, builders, executives, or long-range thinkers trying to understand where AI is actually heading. Regardless of background, the same questions begin to surface once the fundamentals are clear. How inference really works in practice. Who controls the chips.

Where energy limits appear. Why so many AI projects fail. How quantum systems fit into the picture. What could break this thesis. What still matters a decade from now.

The purpose of this appendix is to answer those questions directly.

What follows is a structured question-and-answer reference designed to clarify the AI infrastructure landscape without hype or speculation. The questions progress from foundational concepts to advanced structural concerns, covering inference chips, energy and cooling, data centers, vertical integration, custom silicon, robotics, quantum convergence, security, investment risk, and long-term scale. Each answer is written to stand on its own, allowing this section to be read straight through or used selectively as a reference.

This appendix is not meant to persuade. It is meant to orient.

If the core chapters of this book explain how AI scales, this section explains how that reality is being discussed, tested, and acted upon across the industry. It is included so readers leave with a grounded understanding of the forces shaping artificial intelligence, not just the theory behind them.

You do not need to agree with every answer to benefit from this section. You only need to understand the constraints they describe.

This appendix also serves as a bridge. The questions raised here connect directly to the broader Invest AI series, including work on quantum computing, robotics, crypto infrastructure, and long-term capital cycles. Future Invest AI volumes will expand many of these questions into full frameworks of their own. This section is where those paths begin.

That is what this appendix is for.

1. What are inference chips, and why do they matter more than AI models for investors?

Inference chips are the physical hardware that actually run artificial intelligence in the real world. Models describe what AI knows. Inference chips determine whether that knowledge can be used cheaply, quickly, and at scale.

From an investor perspective, models change fast and become commodities. Hardware takes years to design, manufacture, deploy, and power. The companies that control inference chips control the cost structure of AI. That is why inference chips matter more than the intelligence itself.

---

2. What is AI inference, and how is it different from training?

Training is when an AI model learns from large amounts of data. It is expensive, slow, and happens occasionally. Inference is when that trained model is used to make decisions in real time.

Every time an AI answers a question, recognizes an image,

drives a car, or runs a robot, inference is happening. Training builds the brain. Inference uses the brain. Most of the cost and scaling pressure comes from inference, not training.

---

3. How do inference chips help systems like ChatGPT respond in real time?

When you send a message to ChatGPT, the model has already been trained. The system does not learn from your message in that moment. Instead, an inference chip runs the model on your input and produces an output.

Inference chips are optimized to do this quickly and efficiently. They allow millions of users to interact with AI systems at the same time without long delays. Without inference chips, real-time AI would not be economically viable.

---

4. Where does inference happen today, in the cloud, on devices, or at the edge?

Inference happens everywhere.

Some inference runs in large cloud data centers. Some runs on phones, laptops, cars, cameras, robots, and industrial machines. This is called edge inference.

As AI spreads into the physical world, more inference moves

closer to where decisions are made. This reduces delay, lowers network costs, and improves reliability. The future of AI is not centralized in one place. It is distributed across many surfaces.

---

5. What is the difference between a GPU, an inference ASIC, a TPU, and an NPU?

A GPU is a general-purpose processor originally designed for graphics but widely used for AI. An inference ASIC is a custom chip designed specifically to run AI inference efficiently. A TPU is Google's custom AI chip optimized for its own workloads. An NPU is a neural processing unit, often used in phones and edge devices.

The key difference is specialization. General chips are flexible but expensive to run at scale. Specialized inference chips are cheaper, more efficient, and better suited for always-on workloads.

---

6. Who builds the most important inference chips today, and who is trying to catch up?

Today, NVIDIA dominates inference chips at scale, especially in data centers. Its hardware and software ecosystem are deeply embedded across the AI industry.

Other major players are trying to reduce dependence on

NVIDIA by building custom inference chips. These include Amazon, Google, Microsoft, and Tesla, each designing silicon tailored to their own AI workloads.

---

7. Why is the "GPU tax" becoming a real business problem?

The "GPU tax" refers to the high and rising cost of renting or buying general-purpose AI hardware to run inference. As AI usage grows, these costs compound quickly.

For companies running AI nonstop, hardware expenses can overwhelm margins. This is why many firms are investing in custom inference chips. Owning the hardware reduces long-term costs and gives control over performance and availability.

---

8. What does latency mean, and why does it decide winners in real-time AI?

Latency is the delay between an input and an output. In AI systems, latency determines how quickly a decision can be made.

Low latency is critical for cars, robots, financial systems, and interactive AI. Even small delays can make systems unsafe or unusable. Companies that can run inference closer to the user with minimal delay gain a strong competitive advantage.

---

9. Why do AI agents change the inference chip story?

AI agents do not just answer questions. They observe, decide, act, and repeat. This creates continuous inference loops.

Agentic systems multiply inference demand because they think and act constantly. This dramatically increases hardware, energy, and cost requirements. As agents become more common, inference chips become even more central to AI economics.

---

10. What is the "inference inversion," and why does it matter for the next decade?

Inference inversion describes the shift where the volume of AI computation used for inference exceeds the computation used for training. This marks a structural change in the AI economy.

When inference dominates, cost, power, and deployment matter more than breakthroughs in model training. This inversion is why infrastructure, not intelligence alone, becomes the deciding factor for AI leadership.

11. Why does artificial intelligence turn electricity into a competitive advantage?

Artificial intelligence only works when it is powered. Every inference consumes electricity. When AI runs nonstop across millions of users and machines, energy cost becomes one of the largest operating expenses.

Companies that can access cheap, reliable electricity can run more AI at lower cost. Over time, this advantage compounds. Energy stops being a background utility and becomes a strategic asset.

---

12. Why does inference make energy the first constraint at scale?

Inference is always on. Unlike training, which happens occasionally, inference runs every second a system is active.

As inference volume grows, energy demand grows continuously. Power limits are reached before intelligence limits. If a system cannot be powered reliably, it cannot scale, no matter how good the model is.

---

13. Why is heat a first-order problem for inference chips and data centers?

Every watt of electricity used by a chip becomes heat. As inference chips grow more powerful and are packed more densely, heat builds faster than it can be removed.

Excess heat reduces performance, shortens hardware lifespan, and forces systems to slow down or shut off. Managing heat is not optional. It directly determines how much AI can run in a given space.

---

14. Why are advanced cooling systems becoming strategic infrastructure?

Traditional air cooling is no longer enough for high-density AI hardware. New inference chips generate more heat per square inch than previous generations.

Advanced cooling methods, including liquid cooling, direct-to-chip cooling, and thermal management systems, are now required. The ability to cool hardware efficiently determines whether new AI capacity can even be deployed.

---

15. What is power density, and why does it limit next-generation AI hardware?

Power density refers to how much electricity can be delivered and dissipated within a small physical area.

Modern inference chips require extremely high power density. Many facilities cannot deliver or manage that level of power safely. This creates a hard ceiling on where advanced AI systems can be built and how fast they can expand.

---

16. Why are data center space and grid access becoming scarce?

AI demand has outpaced the ability to build new data centers and expand electrical grids. Securing land, permits, power connections, and cooling infrastructure takes years.

As a result, available space with sufficient power is becoming rare. Companies that plan infrastructure early gain access. Late movers often cannot find capacity at any price.

---

17. What does "power-first site selection" mean, and why is it changing AI geography?

Power-first site selection means choosing locations based primarily on energy availability rather than proximity to users or network hubs.

As AI power needs grow, companies prioritize regions with abundant electricity, stable grids, and room to expand. This is reshaping where AI infrastructure is built and shifting investment away from traditional tech centers.

---

18. What are the real bottlenecks for scaling AI infrastructure?

The main bottlenecks are not just chips. They include power

delivery, cooling capacity, grid upgrades, network bandwidth, manufacturing lead times, and regulatory approval.

These constraints interact. Solving one without the others does not unlock scale. This is why AI infrastructure behaves like heavy industry, not software.

---

19. What does "behind-the-meter energy" mean, and why are AI campuses pursuing it?

Behind-the-meter energy refers to power generated directly for a facility without relying on the public grid. This can include gas turbines, on-site generation, or dedicated energy sources.

AI campuses pursue this approach to secure reliable power, reduce exposure to grid limits, and control long-term energy costs. It is a sign that public infrastructure is no longer sufficient for AI scale.

---

20. What is the AI infrastructure timeline problem, and why does it reshape competition?

AI demand grows faster than infrastructure can be built. Chips, power plants, data centers, and grid upgrades all have long lead times.

Companies that commit early gain capacity years ahead of

competitors. Those that wait may be locked out entirely. This timing mismatch turns infrastructure planning into a decisive competitive advantage.

11. Why does artificial intelligence turn electricity into a competitive advantage?

Artificial intelligence only works when it is powered. Every inference consumes electricity. When AI runs nonstop across millions of users and machines, energy cost becomes one of the largest operating expenses.

Companies that can access cheap, reliable electricity can run more AI at lower cost. Over time, this advantage compounds. Energy stops being a background utility and becomes a strategic asset.

---

12. Why does inference make energy the first constraint at scale?

Inference is always on. Unlike training, which happens occasionally, inference runs every second a system is active.

As inference volume grows, energy demand grows continuously. Power limits are reached before intelligence limits. If a system cannot be powered reliably, it cannot scale, no matter how good the model is.

---

13. Why is heat a first-order problem for inference chips and data centers?

Every watt of electricity used by a chip becomes heat. As inference chips grow more powerful and are packed more densely, heat builds faster than it can be removed.

Excess heat reduces performance, shortens hardware lifespan, and forces systems to slow down or shut off. Managing heat is not optional. It directly determines how much AI can run in a given space.

---

14. Why are advanced cooling systems becoming strategic infrastructure?

Traditional air cooling is no longer enough for high-density AI hardware. New inference chips generate more heat per square inch than previous generations.

Advanced cooling methods, including liquid cooling, direct-to-chip cooling, and thermal management systems, are now required. The ability to cool hardware efficiently determines whether new AI capacity can even be deployed.

---

15. What is power density, and why does it limit next-generation AI hardware?

Power density refers to how much electricity can be delivered and dissipated within a small physical area.

Modern inference chips require extremely high power density. Many facilities cannot deliver or manage that level of power safely. This creates a hard ceiling on where advanced AI systems can be built and how fast they can expand.

---

16. Why are data center space and grid access becoming scarce?

AI demand has outpaced the ability to build new data centers and expand electrical grids. Securing land, permits, power connections, and cooling infrastructure takes years.

As a result, available space with sufficient power is becoming rare. Companies that plan infrastructure early gain access. Late movers often cannot find capacity at any price.

---

17. What does "power-first site selection" mean, and why is it changing AI geography?

Power-first site selection means choosing locations based primarily on energy availability rather than proximity to users or network hubs.

As AI power needs grow, companies prioritize regions with abundant electricity, stable grids, and room to expand. This is reshaping where AI infrastructure is built and shifting investment away from traditional tech centers.

---

18. What are the real bottlenecks for scaling AI infrastructure?

The main bottlenecks are not just chips. They include power delivery, cooling capacity, grid upgrades, network bandwidth, manufacturing lead times, and regulatory approval.

These constraints interact. Solving one without the others does not unlock scale. This is why AI infrastructure behaves like heavy industry, not software.

---

19. What does "behind-the-meter energy" mean, and why are AI campuses pursuing it?

Behind-the-meter energy refers to power generated directly for a facility without relying on the public grid. This can include gas turbines, on-site generation, or dedicated energy sources.

AI campuses pursue this approach to secure reliable power, reduce exposure to grid limits, and control long-term energy costs. It is a sign that public infrastructure is no longer sufficient for AI scale.

---

20. What is the AI infrastructure timeline problem, and why does it reshape competition?

AI demand grows faster than infrastructure can be built. Chips, power plants, data centers, and grid upgrades all have long lead times.

Companies that commit early gain capacity years ahead of competitors. Those that wait may be locked out entirely. This timing mismatch turns infrastructure planning into a decisive competitive advantage.

21. What does vertical integration mean in AI, and why does it beat pure model companies?

Vertical integration in AI means owning multiple layers of the system that runs intelligence. This includes chips, energy access, manufacturing, deployment, and distribution, not just software models.

Pure model companies depend on others for hardware and power. Vertically integrated companies control costs, reliability, and scale. Over time, this control matters more than having the smartest model, because infrastructure advantages compound.

---

22. What is the inference infrastructure stack, and which layers matter most?

The inference infrastructure stack describes everything required to run AI in the real world. It includes silicon, energy, cooling, manufacturing, networking, deployment surfaces, and feedback from reality.

The most important layers are the ones that constrain scale. Chips, power delivery, cooling, and deployment usually matter more than software features because they determine whether intelligence can run at all.

---

23. What is the "control plane" in inference, and why does it become a moat?

The control plane is the system that orchestrates how inference workloads are distributed across hardware, locations, and time. It decides which chips run which tasks, when, and at what cost.

As AI systems grow more complex, orchestration becomes as important as raw compute. Companies that can manage inference as a unified fabric gain efficiency, lower costs, and resilience. This coordination layer becomes a durable advantage.

---

24. Why are hyperscalers building custom silicon, and will it reduce dependence on NVIDIA?

Large cloud and AI companies are building custom inference chips to lower long-term costs and avoid relying entirely on external suppliers like NVIDIA.

Custom silicon will reduce some dependence, but it will not eliminate it quickly. NVIDIA's ecosystem, software stack, and manufacturing scale remain difficult to replace. The likely outcome is diversification, not full displacement.

---

25. How does manufacturing capacity become an AI advantage?

Designing chips is only part of the challenge. Manufacturing them at scale requires access to advanced fabrication, long-term supply contracts, and complex logistics.

Companies with guaranteed manufacturing capacity can deploy AI faster and more reliably. Those without it face delays, shortages, and higher costs. Manufacturing turns AI from a software race into an industrial one.

---

26. What role do satellites and space networks play in inference scale?

Satellites extend connectivity and computation to places traditional networks cannot reach. They can support distributed inference for vehicles, sensors, and global systems.

Space does not replace terrestrial data centers, but it expands the inference surface. In certain use cases, global coverage and low-latency access matter more than centralized efficiency.

---

27. What is sovereign AI, and why does it matter?

Sovereign AI refers to a nation's ability to run artificial intelligence using domestic infrastructure rather than relying entirely on foreign platforms.

Governments care about data control, security, and resilience. This pushes investment into local data centers, energy systems, and chips. Sovereign AI fragments the global AI landscape and reshapes where infrastructure is built.

---

28. How does quantum computing connect to AI inference and training?

Quantum computing is not a replacement for classical inference chips. Instead, it is expected to act as a specialized accelerator for optimization problems.

Quantum systems may help design better models, optimize energy use, improve materials, and reduce training complexity. Inference itself is likely to remain classical, but optimized by quantum-assisted processes.

---

29. What is the qRAM or data-loading bottleneck, and why does it matter?

Quantum systems require data to be loaded into quantum memory, a process that is technically difficult and resource-intensive. This is known as the qRAM bottleneck.

If data cannot be loaded efficiently, quantum advantages shrink. This bottleneck is a major reason why hybrid quantum-classical systems are more realistic than pure quantum AI in the near term.

---

30. What could break the inference chip thesis?

Several factors could weaken or delay the thesis. Regulatory limits could restrict deployment. Geopolitical conflict could disrupt supply chains. New computing paradigms could change cost structures. Cloud providers could regain control through pricing power.

The thesis does not assume certainty. It assumes that physical constraints matter. If those constraints change, the framework adapts.

31. Why do so many AI projects fail despite massive investment?

Most AI projects fail because they focus on models instead of infrastructure. Teams build impressive prototypes without securing the power, hardware, cooling, and deployment workflows needed to run them reliably.

When AI moves from demos to production, hidden costs appear. Latency increases. Energy bills spike. Systems become unstable. Without infrastructure planning, intelligence cannot translate into value.

---

32. Why is return on investment becoming the central AI question?

AI infrastructure now requires billions in capital. Boards and executives are no longer satisfied with experimentation.

The question has shifted from "What can this model do?" to "What does it cost to run this every day?" Inference economics determine whether AI becomes a profit center or a permanent expense.

---

33. How do inference chips change the economics of AI agents and robotics?

AI agents and robots require constant inference to observe, decide, and act. This creates a continuous cost stream.

Inference chips optimized for efficiency reduce operating costs and enable scale. Without them, agentic systems become too expensive to deploy broadly. Hardware efficiency determines whether autonomy is affordable.

---

34. Why does depreciation risk matter for AI hardware investors?

AI hardware improves quickly. Chips purchased today may be outperformed within a few years.

Investors must consider not just performance but lifespan, resale value, and upgrade paths. Companies that control their own silicon and deployment cycles manage depreciation better than those reliant on external suppliers.

---

35. How does AI infrastructure create feedback loops that compound advantage?

When inference runs on owned hardware, data flows directly back into optimization. Systems improve efficiency, reliability, and cost over time.

These feedback loops compound. Each deployment strengthens the next. This is why infrastructure advantages widen rather than narrow as AI scales.

---

36. What role does robotics play in the future inference economy?

Robots turn inference into physical action. Every movement, correction, and decision requires compute.

As robotics expands, inference demand multiplies. The companies that can power robots cheaply and reliably gain leverage across logistics, manufacturing, and services. Robotics accelerates the infrastructure thesis.

---

37. How does quantum computing affect AI security and long-term risk?

Quantum computing threatens current encryption standards. Data encrypted today could be decrypted in the future.

This creates pressure to redesign security systems alongside AI infrastructure. Companies and governments must plan for quantum-safe architectures while scaling inference, adding another layer of complexity and cost.

---

38. What does the AI landscape likely look like by 2036?

By 2036, fewer companies will control most AI infrastructure. Intelligence will be widespread, but the ability to run it cheaply will be concentrated.

AI systems will resemble utilities. Regions will develop their own AI stacks. Infrastructure ownership will matter more than brand or model performance.

---

39. How should investors think about positioning across the AI stack?

Investors should separate hype from structure. Direct exposure offers upside but carries risk. Derivative exposure benefits from scale regardless of winners. Picks-and-shovels provide durability.

Understanding where inference costs concentrate helps identify where value compounds and where margins erode.

---

40. What is the single most important takeaway from this book?

Artificial intelligence does not scale on intelligence alone. It scales on chips, power, heat management, manufacturing, and deployment.

Whoever controls inference infrastructure controls the AI economy. This reality shapes outcomes whether markets acknowledge it or not.

15

Conclusion

Artificial intelligence did not fail to become intelligent.

It failed to become cheap, stable, and everywhere all at once.

That is the misunderstanding that shaped the last wave of AI thinking. Intelligence was treated as the finish line. In reality, intelligence was the starting point. Once models reached a certain level of capability, the problem stopped being what AI could do and became whether the world could afford to run it.

This book began with inference chips for a reason.

Inference is where artificial intelligence leaves theory and enters the physical world. It is where costs appear. It is where energy is consumed. It is where heat accumulates. It is where delays matter. It is where reliability becomes non-negotiable. Intelligence that cannot survive these conditions does not scale, no matter how impressive it looks in isolation.

From there, the logic compounds.

Always-on inference turns energy into a governing constraint.

Energy constraints reward vertical integration.

Vertical integration reshapes competition.

Infrastructure ownership outlasts model advantage.

Budgets decide outcomes long before intelligence does.

By the time artificial intelligence reaches into vehicles, factories, logistics systems, cities, and orbit, it no longer behaves like software. It behaves like infrastructure. And infrastructure follows different rules.

It scales slowly. It compounds quietly. It favors owners over renters. It punishes inefficiency.

This is why the same companies keep appearing across seemingly unrelated parts of the AI landscape. Not because they share a vision, but because they are responding to the same physical limits. Chips, power, deployment, manufacturing, cooling, permission, and feedback from reality are not optional layers. They are the system.

The Invest AI Budget Stack is not a prediction. It is an accounting.

Energy, heat, permission, and reality do not care about narratives. They do not move faster because markets are excited. They do not bend to intelligence alone. Any AI system that ignores one of these budgets eventually stalls, no matter how advanced it appears on paper.

This is why this book does not attempt to name winners.

The future of AI will not be decided by a single company, model, or announcement. It will be decided by which organizations can build and operate intelligence within real constraints, over long periods of time, at a scale that the world can sustain.

For investors, this changes the question.

The question is no longer which model is smartest.

The question is where intelligence becomes affordable, reliable, and unavoidable.

The question is who owns the machinery that makes that possible.

This book was written to provide orientation, not certainty.

You can disagree with parts of it and still use the framework. You can forget the details and still remember the structure. You can return to it when headlines change and ask the same simple question again.

Can this intelligence run everywhere, all the time, without breaking the system that supports it?

If the answer is no, the story is not finished. If the answer is yes, the outcome is already in motion.

That is how the inference era should be read.

And that is where this book ends.

www.ingramcontent.com/pod-product-compliance
Lightning Source LLC
LaVergne TN
LVHW090427210926
848480LV00002B/723
* 9 7 9 8 2 9 5 6 1 5 8 7 0 *